LITTLE
LEAP
FORWARD

A BOY IN BEIJING

by

Guo Yue and Clare Farrow

Illustrated by Helen Cann

Barefoot Books
step inside a story

CONTENTS

CHAPTER ONE
THE DRUM AND BELL TOWERS
7

CHAPTER TWO
MY FRIEND LITTLE-LITTLE
13

CHAPTER THREE
WHITE PAPER KITES
23

CHAPTER FOUR
LITTLE CLOUD
31

CHAPTER FIVE
RED SILK RIBBONS
43

LITTLE
LEAP
FORWARD

A BOY IN BEIJING

To our children – Y. G. and C. F.

Barefoot Books
294 Banbury Road
Oxford OX2 7ED

First published in Great Britain in 2008 by Barefoot Books, Ltd
This paperback edition published in 2011

This book has been printed on 100% acid-free paper

Graphic design by Graham Webb, Warminster
and Penny Lamprell, Lymington
Colour separation by B & P International, Hong Kong
Printed and bound in China by Printplus, Ltd

This book was typeset in Carmina
The illustrations were prepared in watercolour and mixed media
on Arches hot press 300gms paper

Paperback ISBN 978-1-84686-538-1

British Cataloguing-in-Publication Data:
a catalogue record for this book is available from the British Library

3 5 7 9 8 6 4 2

CHAPTER SIX
BLUE'S COURTYARD
53

CHAPTER SEVEN
MY BAMBOO FLUTE
71

CHAPTER EIGHT
THE RED GUARDS
83

CHAPTER NINE
INTO THE SKY
97

CHAPTER TEN
AUTUMN SONG
109

AFTERWORD
115

CHAPTER ONE

THE DRUM AND BELL TOWERS

WHEN I WAS A LITTLE BOY, I lived in an old courtyard in Beijing, China, between the Drum Tower, the Bell Tower and the river. My home was in the poor and overcrowded hutongs – a maze of dark, narrow alleys and high brick walls, with grey earth on the ground and big wooden gates leading into courtyards. You had to look up and up to see the sky. Some gates had old stone lions guarding them, and sloping roofs with tiles shaped like waves.

'The workers of the Emperor used to live here, Little Leap Forward, five hundred years ago,' my mother told me, 'and the huge drum and bell in the towers used to sound every hour.'

I imagined the Emperors' workers, like bees in a hive, filling the alleys with the scent of honey.

'Did you know that bees dance, Ma?' I asked her.

'Do they?' my mother answered, a smile flickering in her dark eyes, making them shine.

'Yes,' I continued, 'and Ma, I think silkworms dance too, but very slowly, when they are making their silk. I have watched them.'

My mother burst out laughing.

'I think you have a very vivid imagination, Little Leap Forward!' she said.

The Drum and Bell Towers had been silent since my mother was a little girl in the 1920s, when the last Emperor of China had lost his power and his title, and people in the alleys had modern clocks for the first time in their homes. My mother had her own very special clock – from Russia. It was made of clear crystal. I liked to see the tiny wheels turning inside, measuring time. But how much more wonderful, I thought, to feel the power of the massive drum and bell, sounding through the alleys.

Inside our small, traditional courtyard, in a long low building with many doors, I lived in two rooms with my mother, brother and four older sisters. Four other families lived in the same building in our courtyard, and they were all musicians. My father had been a musician too: he had played the Chinese violin. When I was very little I had watched him rehearse in the big modern courtyard not far from our home, where many of the musicians in his orchestra lived and where they practised. It was full of cherry trees that blossomed in the spring and a mulberry tree that I often climbed when I was older, to collect leaves for my silkworms to eat. I kept these tiny artists in a box in our inner room, where we kept all our special things.

My father's violin had two strings, a bow made of horses' hair, and a dragon's head carved on the top. He could make this instrument sound like horses neighing and galloping on the Mongolian grasslands.

'Just remember,' he once said to me, as he made a red boiled sweet appear as if by magic out of the red silk velvet lining of his violin case, 'with music and

your imagination you can travel anywhere; you will always be free.'

My father had died two years before, when I was five, nearly six years old.

'Do I look like Baba?' I asked my mother, as she sat sewing in the dim light of our outer room one evening, after she had returned from her work as a teacher.

'Let me look at you,' she said, taking my face in her beautiful hands.

'Yes. Yes, there is something, in those deep brown eyes, and in the corners of your mouth when you smile – there is something that reminds me of him.'

'I'm going to be a musician too, Ma!' I said.

'Are you, Little Leap Forward? And will you write music for your silkworms to dance to?' She looked steadily into my eyes, and I felt a rush of love for her.

'Little Leap Forward,' my sister Swallow called from the courtyard. 'Come and wash the vegetables!'

Lowering her head, my mother returned to the blue padded jacket she was mending, moving the big needle slowly through the thick cotton material.

CHAPTER TWO

MY FRIEND
LITTLE-LITTLE

MY BEST FRIEND WAS CALLED Little-Little. He lived in our courtyard with his mother and father (a musician from the countryside), and his younger brother Little Stone. Little-Little was like a brown bear-cub. His hair was cut so short that it gleamed like velvet in the sun and his black eyes were bright and mischievous. He was full of a kind of tumbling energy, moving from one idea to the next like a cricket leaping through the long grass.

Dressed in our white vests, blue cotton jackets and trousers, like every child in the alleys, we looked like brothers; though my friend Little-Little didn't agree.

'Your face is so pale, my mother says you look like a Russian!' he laughed. 'This is what comes of watching your silkworms all night. Come on "white-flour-face" – I'll race you to the river!'

Running through the narrow alleys we would dodge the many bicycles and the women carrying straw baskets or painted metal washing-basins with vegetables from the grocery shop. Five minutes later we were flinging ourselves on to the brown earth of the riverbank, out of breath and gazing up into the blue sky. I always thought that the river and the wheat-fields across the wooden bridge were really Little-Little's home. He seemed to belong there.

The earth smelt fresh and damp beside the river, even in the heat of summer, and you could hear the wind rustling the heart-shaped leaves of the Yang Shu trees, whose snow-white trunks soared straight up into the sky. I was happy to lie on the riverbank, listening to the birds singing in the branches above my head. I liked to imagine that I was one of them; so light that I could fling myself suddenly into the huge blueness of the sky.

'Do you think birds always sing the same notes, Little-Little? Or do they sing different songs at different times?'

'I don't know,' my friend answered, closing his eyes. 'You could write the notes down and see.'

We lay there, feeling part of the sky.

'Do you think they can choose which notes to sing?' I asked him.

'No,' said Little-Little. 'They just sing the music that's inside them. That's all they can do. It's as simple as that.'

'I don't know,' I replied. 'I don't think it's so simple.'

I could feel my mind drifting like the clouds. We were silent for a few minutes.

'Do you think birds get as hungry as we do, Leap Forward?' Little-Little suddenly asked.

I had trained myself not to think too much about food: only when my sisters sent me running down the alley to the grocery shop to buy vegetables, or when I watched them cooking and singing in the evenings. I didn't think about it at other times. I was always too hungry.

'Only in the winter,' I replied, 'when they can't reach the earth through the snow. In the summer they have as many berries, worms and seeds as they like. They don't need ration tickets like we do, and they don't have my sisters measuring their food with a ruler!'

Little-Little laughed. 'And they don't have to spend all that time heating up a coal stove!' he said.

I thought about waiting in the evening for my mother to come home from work, and watching my sisters measuring out the rice from a small white sack that they guarded like treasure, because it had to last the entire month. There was never enough to fill you up. I thought about my father before he died – how he had asked my mother for an egg or a fresh apple to eat, but she couldn't give him either. Many people had died in China at that time – because there wasn't enough food. 'But things are getting better

now, Little Leap Forward,' my mother had said to me, smoothing my hair with her fingers. 'I will try to get some pears tomorrow, and perhaps some noodles too.'

I looked across at Little-Little. His eyes were still closed.

'Let's talk about something else,' I said.

'Ok,' he said. 'But you think of something.'

I stared up through the pattern of green leaves and listened to the birds singing again.

'My sister Swallow says the Russians will soon be sending people to the moon,' I told him. 'Can you believe it? Would you go, Little-Little, if you had the chance?'

'Sure,' he said, opening his eyes wide and grinning. 'I'd travel anywhere. The moon, the stars!'

'Do you think you can see the Drum and Bell Towers from the moon?' I continued seriously.

'Yes, Leap Forward – and you can also see a crazy boy with no shoes!' he laughed, pulling off my black cotton shoes and throwing them to the other side of the riverbank. I jumped up and pushed him, laughing.

'I know!' he said, kicking off his own shoes and rolling his trousers up to his knees. 'Let's see who can catch a fish!'

The water was clear and cold as we stood side by side in the river.

'They know we're here,' Little-Little whispered. 'They think if they hide in the shadows for long enough, we'll go away. You have to be completely still. You have to play the same trick on them.'

I watched the water lapping the stones. The river had been made in the Ming Dynasty, when Beijing became the capital of China, when the Drum and Bell Towers were built, and poets and artists filled the streets of the city. Had any of them stood on these stones?

There was a sudden rush of water as Little-Little thrust his hands into the river. His face was red with excitement.

'Look Leap Forward!'

A little brown fish lay in the deep lines of his palm. He had made a bowl with his hands.

'Well done! But it's not much of a mouthful, is it?' I laughed.

'No, you're right,' he replied, squinting with amusement at the fish. 'Here, you have it. I'm going to skim some stones.'

I took the fish from him and felt the strength of its life in my hands. Its eyes were dark and shining, and its mouth was moving with a gentle rhythm even though, at that moment, it was fighting for breath. I stroked its shining body with the side of my thumb: there were little spots and stripes of gold on its skin, and its fins were transparent like glass in the sunlight. I only had to clench my fist and it would die. Could it feel my strength, I wondered?

I thought about the goldfish that I kept in a glass tank in our inner room – bright orange like paintings, with tails as fine as white silk fans. But this tiny fish was somehow more beautiful – more delicate. I bent down and opened my hands in the water. The fish was still for a second, and then it darted back into the shadows of the stones.

'Come on, Leap Forward,' my friend shouted. 'I've found enough flat stones to have a competition!'

CHAPTER THREE

WHITE PAPER KITES

O F THE MANY GAMES WE PLAYED, our favourite was to make and fly kites. First we needed paper, and my mother's writing paper was just right. In our outer room, we had a wooden chest with many drawers, which my mother had acquired from a tiny shop, near the Drum Tower, that sold all kinds of traditional Chinese teas, among them her favourite, Jasmine-flower tea. It was made of walnut wood, my mother said, and shone when she rubbed it with a piece of cloth.

This chest had twenty-seven little drawers, which my family used for storing everything: from paperclips, pencils and rubber bands, to fresh ginger, garlic and star anise, which my sisters used to flavour their cooking. In the middle, at the top, was one larger drawer in which my mother kept her writing paper – crisp white paper with thin red lines printed on it, known in China as 'message paper'. Having been kept in that drawer, the paper always carried the light, beautiful fragrance of High Mountain tea.

I talked with Little-Little as we mixed a bit of flour and water together in a cup to make glue.

'In the old days, before Chairman Mao, people used to write messages or poetry on the tails of their kites, and paint flowers and dragons on the paper. Imagine how amazing they looked in the sky, Little-Little,' I said. 'My mother remembers flying them in the winter with her Russian friends, when she was a little girl. They all wore fur coats, so they didn't feel the cold. And the girls wore different coloured skirts and fur muffs to keep their hands warm. My mother says it was beautiful to see all the different colours spinning round and round, making shapes and patterns on the ice.

'But Mao says it was wrong for people to live like that, Leap Forward,' Little-Little said, testing the glue with his finger. 'We should live like peasants – be good Communists.'

He pulled at a loose button on his blue jacket.

'Anyway, I think our kites are the best in the world,' he said. 'Who needs flowers and dragons, like Emperors and Russian Tsars? Our kites can fly as high as the clouds – just as they are!'

I nodded, and went back to making our kites. But still, secretly, I loved my mother's stories. I liked to imagine a different, more colourful world. Taking two bamboo sticks, cut to the right length, we stuck them on to a sheet of paper, like a cross. Then we cut narrow strips of paper and glued them, end to end, to make long, floating tails, which we fixed on to our kites.

Finally we attached a long string, with a bamboo bobbin on the end. With this, you could wind or unwind the string – like the bobbin on a sewing machine. My favourite moment was when I carried my kite outside, through the courtyard and out into the alley. If the wind was strong, the kite would already begin to wriggle in my hands.

'It wants to play,' Little-Little would say.

'Look, Little Leap Forward. You see how the word "kite" is written as two characters,' my mother explained to me one morning. I watched her bamboo brush dancing across the page, leaving ribbons of black ink arranged neatly on the red printed lines. 'The first character is "wind", the second means "bamboo struggle". Do you see? It is like poetry. It paints a picture in your imagination.'

A loose strand of hair had fallen across my mother's cheek as she handed the brush to me. I wondered if there was a character to describe that. I turned the brush in a circle on the wet ink-stone, and began to copy her characters with my left hand, sweeping my brush clumsily across the paper. This wasn't poetry, I thought. Poetry was the sound of the river and the birds singing in the

Yang Shu trees. Not black ink and red lines.

'Leap Forward, are you coming to the river?' Little-Little's voice sounded like a trumpet outside in the courtyard.

I looked up at my mother, who shook her head and smiled. 'Perhaps you will be a different sort of poet,' she said. 'Go and play by the river. But don't bring any more crickets home to hide under my bed!'

I ran outside into the courtyard, and found Little-Little sitting on the step, eating a slice of watermelon and spitting the pips onto the ground. The sweet red juice was running down his chin, as he looked up at me and grinned.

'I've got the best plan, Leap Forward. Come on. You carry this,' he said, picking up a metal washing-basin and thrusting it into my hands. It was painted white and the inside was decorated with a design of pale pink cherry blossom.

'You're going to buy vegetables?' I asked him, surprised by his obvious excitement.

Shaking his head, he waved a red lacquer chopstick

and a long piece of string in front of my face, picked up a little cardboard box, and marched out of the courtyard, into the crowded alley.

'You're going to catch a fish?' I continued, running after him.

'The trouble with you, Leap Forward,' he said, trying to look serious, 'is that you have no patience. I have often noted that!'

At which point, he bolted like a wild rabbit down a narrow alley, and we raced each other to the river.

CHAPTER FOUR

LITTLE CLOUD

'YOU HAVE TO BE AS CUNNING AS A spider weaving its web,' Little-Little whispered, setting up his things with the methodical care of a musician fitting a wind instrument together. He pushed the chopstick into the brown earth of the riverbank until it stood as straight and firm as a tree trunk. Then he turned the washing-basin upside down and balanced one side on the end of the chopstick. It looked like a funny kind of hat. Then he tied the string to the bottom of the chopstick, just above the ground, and slowly unwound it, walking carefully backwards as he did so. Leaving the end of the string on the earth, he returned to the washing-basin and, taking a few grains of rice out of his pocket, scattered them on to the ground. Holding the end of the string, he lay down on the riverbank beside me, his eyes fixed on the rice beneath the basin.

We lay there for a long time, our bodies pressed against the damp earth.

'Little-Little,' I whispered. 'What are we doing?'

'Just be quiet, Leap Forward, and you'll see!'

'Have you been drinking your father's rice wine?' I asked him. 'Or have you just gone mad?'

'Shh,' my friend replied, keeping his dark eyes fixed on the rice. 'You have to be quiet.'

I looked at Little-Little. He was as still as stone, hardly even breathing. Suddenly, his whole body stiffened. 'Look!'

At that moment, a tiny yellow bird danced lightly across the earth towards the rice, and then stood in the shadow of the basin, pecking at the tiny grains. With a sudden movement of his hand, Little-Little pulled the string, bringing the washing-basin down and trapping the bird inside it.

We ran towards the basin and Little-Little pushed his hand carefully underneath it, bringing out the bird and clasping it in his hands.

'I think my heart is beating faster than the bird's,' he laughed.

'Well done Little-Little!' I congratulated him. 'But what are you going to do with it?'

'It's for you!' he laughed. 'You wanted to know how a bird sings. So now you have one! You can keep it in the courtyard. Build a little cage – you're good at that kind of thing. It can be a friend for your silkworms and goldfish. Here, take it! I want to play in the river.'

'Thanks Little-Little!' I said.

I put my hands over his, and took the tiny bird from him. Her feathers were unbelievably soft. She was so light and motionless; so fragile, except for the rapid beating of her heart, which throbbed against my palm like a little drum. I could sense her fear, pressing into my hands. Her eyes were dark and bright; and I could feel the tension in her body, like the string of a violin, just before it breaks. She was so beautiful. I didn't want to hurt her.

I walked over to the cardboard box and opened one flap, putting her gently inside and closing the top. There was a narrow gap in the cardboard, which allowed air into the box.

I looked up and saw Little-Little happily skimming stones. I knew his mind was already on other things.

'See you in the courtyard,' he shouted.

I trod carefully with the precious box in my arms, through the narrow alleys towards my home. It was like carrying nothing – the box was so light – and yet I knew there was treasure inside. By the time I reached my courtyard, I could no longer see the open sky: just a web of electricity wires weaving between the grey brick walls of the alleys and buildings. The little bird had been still and silent all the way; but now I could feel her wings fluttering like a trapped butterfly against the cardboard walls of the box.

'It's all right,' I whispered. 'We're home now. I'm going to look after you.'

My sister Swallow was standing in our outer room, with a red washing-basin at her feet. Inside were tomatoes, potatoes and aubergines.

'Where have you been, Leap Forward?' she asked impatiently. 'I was calling you. Here, go and wash these vegetables and then bring them inside.'

She picked up the red basin and then gave me a quizzical look.

'What have you got in that box? Isn't it enough to have seven people in two rooms, without bringing the entire riverbank to live here too?'

When her question met with silence, she softened her voice.

'Well, never mind. You can show me later.'

I pushed the cardboard box under my bed and carried the heavy basin outside. Standing under the big tree in the courtyard, I turned on the tap of icy-cold water and began to wash the vegetables, which had arrived that morning on horse-drawn carts from the countryside. I didn't mind washing the tomatoes and aubergines, which soon gleamed like red and purple jewels under the water; but I hated washing the earth from the potatoes, and I could feel my fingers going numb as I rubbed the skins to get them clean.

Inside, my sister was busy opening little drawers in the wooden chest, removing brown paper packages and sorting bottles like a magician preparing for a spell.

'Here, Little Leap Forward. Let me see how well you can chop a potato today. I want you to cut it into matchsticks. Make sure they are all the same length: then the dish will taste good.'

I took the potato from her hand. She had already peeled it and cut it in half. Holding the knife in my left hand, I began cutting thin slices on the wooden board. Then I arranged these slices like the pages of a book, one on top of the other, and slowly chopped them into very thin sticks of potato. I loved the way these sticks fell onto the board, transformed from hard potato into fine strands that were like silk to touch. My sister prepared the other potatoes in the same way.

'Well done, Leap Forward. Now, since we don't have any pork today, shall we chop those little Buddha earlobes to make an even tastier dish?'

I put my hands over my ears and laughed. My thick, curved earlobes were thought to be very lucky.

I stood back and watched my sister heating the wok on our coal stove and drizzling a little of our precious peanut oil inside. Many of our ingredients were still rationed, after the years of famine in China: meat, fish, eggs, sugar, wheat flour, rice, bean curd, peanut and sesame seed oil. Each family could only have a little of these each month, so we valued them very much.

In the winter we had to eat a lot of pickled vegetables, potatoes and cabbage, which was piled high in the snowy courtyards. But in the summer there were fresh, colourful things to buy with our ration tickets. 'Fresh tomatoes and cucumbers are here today!' people would shout down the alley, and a long queue would immediately form outside the grocery shop.

When the oil was hot and beginning to smoke, Swallow added some finely chopped spring onion, which made a whooshing sound, followed by the potato, which made a dramatic sound like a clash of cymbals. Then came the magical bit: a tiny sprinkling of white sugar from one parcel, a few pinches of crushed rock salt from another, a drizzle of soy sauce from one bottle and dark rice vinegar from another, and finally, three drops of sesame seed oil, like liquid gold, from another. The air was filled with a delicious perfume. She tipped the silky potato into a blue and white patterned dish, and then turned her attention to the tomatoes and aubergines.

'Everyone should be home soon, Leap Forward. Go and get the chopsticks from the drawer.'

Later that evening, I sat down to talk to my mother who was marking her students' papers with a sharp yellow pencil.

'Ma, can I show you something? Something very special?'

She looked up at me in surprise.

'What is it, Leap Forward?' she asked.

I ran to get the cardboard box. I put my hands in quickly, grasping the tiny bird and feeling the strength of her wings pressing against me. I whistled gently to comfort her, and my breath ruffled the feathers on her head. My mother stroked her softly with the tip of her little finger.

'Well, she's a lot prettier than a cricket,' she laughed, 'but more difficult to look after too. What are you going to do with her?'

'I'm going to make a house for her in the court-yard, and give her grain to eat, and I'm going to write down the notes she sings and whistle them so she will answer me.'

'I think you really are a musician,' my mother smiled. 'But just make sure you never forget about her. If you keep her in the courtyard she will need you to do everything for her. She is not a toy. You must give her fresh food and water every day.'

'Yes Ma, I will look after her very well. And Ma, I was thinking of calling her Little Cloud. What do you think?'

'I think it's a beautiful name, Leap Forward. Now run along, I have to finish these papers before tomorrow,' she said, picking up the yellow pencil and tapping it thoughtfully on the table.

CHAPTER FIVE

RED SILK RIBBONS

I N MY SCHOOL, WHICH WAS HOUSED IN an old temple courtyard near the river, with high-ceilinged rooms that were cool even in the summer, I boasted about my bird the following day.

'I'm going to train her to sit on my hand and sing,' I said.

'Are you going to teach her all the revolutionary songs about Chairman Mao?' my friend Red-Red laughed.

We knew all these songs by heart – old tunes, often love songs, which had been given new, revolutionary words, about our leader Mao Zedong and his Red Army. These were the only songs we were allowed to sing. The most famous one was 'The East is Red'.

'Very funny,' I replied. 'I want to write down the notes that she sings. I'm going to study her music.'

'My father says that keeping birds in cages is old-fashioned,' another boy said.

'You'll be like those old men who carry their bird-cages to the park and hang them from trees while they play Chinese chess!' laughed another.

A bell rang and we sat down in our rows of wooden desks to begin lessons. Everything in our classroom was in straight lines. I opened the lid of my desk. Inside was the ink-stone and calligraphy brush that my mother had bought me from the Red Flag Paper Shop, and two red pencils that I liked to sharpen to a very fine point. The teacher was handing round sheets of rice paper, which had red squares printed on it: one square for each character.

'"Feng" (Wind),' announced the teacher, and we all wrote the character for 'wind' in our first red square.

'Leap Forward! You must use your right hand, not your left hand, for writing. Don't let me see you doing that again.'

I put the brush into my right hand, and turned it in a circle on the wet ink stone. But I couldn't control the brush with my right hand, and I smudged the ink on the paper.

'Leap Forward, each character must stay inside the red square. Now repeat the exercise until you get it right.'

I looked up at the big wooden beams, which supported the high ceiling of this old temple. In the past, people had prayed there, before Chairman Mao had banned religion in China.

'What did they pray for?' I once asked my mother.

'They prayed for good harvests, so the people would have food to eat. They prayed for the people they loved, or if they had questions that could not be answered.'

'What if I have questions that cannot be answered, Ma?' I asked her.

My mother thought for a moment, and then replied:

'Go to the river, Leap Forward. If you sit very

quietly with nature, then sometimes you will find the answers.'

My gaze wandered to the girl who was sitting at the desk in front of me, writing with her brush on the rice paper.

'"Tian" (Sky),' announced the teacher, writing the Chinese character in strong white chalk on the large blackboard at the front of the class. The girl bent her head down in concentration. She had two long black plaits, each tied with a red silk ribbon in a bow. Her name was Lan, meaning Blue. I thought she was like a painting. I reached out with my foot, under my desk, trying to touch her black cotton shoes. But she took no notice of me. And so I thought about my bird, and how I should design a house for her in the courtyard.

'Leap Forward!' the teacher announced. 'You are supposed to be writing "Sky", not looking at it!'

I bent my head down to the paper. But I held on to my thoughts.

When I got home, I found my first sister's

boyfriend, whose name was Clear Waves, cleaning his bicycle in the courtyard. He was from the countryside, and was very practical. He had never read a book, but was very good at making things with his hands. He had made three wooden shelves for my mother's books and a box for her sewing things. His bicycle was a dark shining blue colour and had little red flags painted all over it. My other sisters used to joke that he loved this bicycle so much he would cover it with his own blanket in the winter! I knew he was very different to my father, but I liked to have a man to talk to.

'Clear Waves, will you help me make a house for my bird?'

'A bird now, is it? Are you not busy enough with your silkworms and goldfish?' he laughed.

'Please, Clear Waves. I want to make her happy. I've been keeping her in a cardboard box for two days and she hasn't sung a note yet. But if she could be outside in the courtyard I think she would be happier.'

Clear Waves kept polishing his bicycle, breathing on it to make the flags shine more brightly.

'Very well, Leap Forward. I will get some bamboo sticks, and we will see what we can do. I'll see you in the courtyard tomorrow afternoon.'

'Thank you!' I said, and ran off to take another look at Little Cloud. I had discovered that she liked man-tou – steamed white bread rolls; although my sisters disapproved whenever I gave her a little of mine.

'White flour is rationed in Beijing, and here you are giving your precious steamed bread to a bird!'

I also discovered that she liked sunflower seeds and certain berries too, which I found for her.

The next afternoon, Clear Waves helped me to make the best cage out of bamboo sticks.

'See how the bamboo bends but never breaks, Leap Forward,' he said, fitting the ends of the sticks into a sequence of little holes at either end of the cage, so it was like a curved lantern. In the bottom we put some straw and Clear Waves tied two little cups to the side: one for food, the other for water. We even fixed a bamboo perch, like the branch of a tree, inside the cage. It was perfect for Little Cloud. When I put her inside, she seemed to dance over the straw and then settled on the perch, her dark eyes bright and alert. I could now see her properly. We made a wire handle and then hung the cage from the lowest branch of the big tree in the corner of our courtyard. I asked everyone to come and admire it.

'Well done Little Leap Forward. It is a work of art,' my mother said. And Clear Waves drank a cup of rice wine in honour of Little Cloud.

Only Little-Little seemed uncertain, and simply shrugged his approval before running off into the alley. But I didn't care. I was proud of the cage, and of the tiny wild bird inside it. I was going to train her to sit on my hand. She was going to sing and I was going to write down her music. She made the courtyard beautiful, like a golden light shining against the old grey bricks. I loved her.

CHAPTER SIX

BLUE'S COURTYARD

'LEAP FORWARD,' SHOUTED LITTLE-LITTLE from the courtyard, 'there's a really strong wind today. We're going to have a kite competition by the river. Three o'clock. You'd better start making a good one, otherwise I'm going to beat you!'

I'd just come back from the grocery shop, with a straw basket of vegetables that my sister Whirlwind had instructed me to buy. I didn't mind standing in the queue, with the pink and green ration tickets in my hand. I liked listening to the conversations around me – usually about food – and watching the care with which people chose their vegetables. They studied a tomato as if it were a work of art in valuable painted red lacquer, or a cucumber as if it were a green jade flute. I too had learnt how to choose the best vegetables: for me, colour was the most important thing, and a fresh, earthy smell that took me out of the alleys and into the countryside that I had never seen.

'I'll be there,' I called out of the door. 'But I have to feed Little Cloud first.'

I put the basket down on the table, and opened one of the many little drawers in the wooden chest. I put my hand in, and took out a few sunflower seeds, which Little Cloud loved to eat. Closing the drawer, I went outside again, and found Little-Little peering into the bamboo cage.

'So she hasn't sung yet, Leap Forward? Maybe birds don't sing in cages after all. I wouldn't! It would be like never being allowed out of this courtyard. I'd go mad!'

'Of course birds sing in cages. Otherwise people wouldn't keep them. She's just getting used to life here, that's all,' I replied impatiently. 'But she does know me,' I continued. 'Watch.'

I went up to her cage and whistled to her, trying to imitate the pattern of notes I had heard beside the river. I held out a seed to her, through one of the spaces in the bamboo. She looked at me with her bright dark eyes, and then with a flutter of her wings, she took the seed from between my fingers.

'But her feathers look a bit faded to me, Leap Forward. Don't you think so?'

'It's just because the sunlight was reflected in the river when you first saw her; everything looks brighter there. Here it's all grey bricks and shadows. But she'll get used to it. I know she will.'

Little-Little looked at me, and shrugged.

'I'm off to make my kite,' he said. 'I bet mine will fly higher than yours!'

He marched into his outer room and closed the door.

The sky was greyer than usual beside the river, but there were still flashes of blue, as dragonflies skimmed the surface of the water, looking for insects. I held my new kite carefully, the six tails rattling and dancing in the wind. There was a group of children from my class, some holding kites, others who had simply come to watch. Among them was Blue. She was wearing a white cotton shirt with blue cotton trousers. She looked so beautiful. I wanted to impress her, to show her that my kite was the best.

'Right,' said Little-Little, calling the chattering group to order.

'Little Stone, Red-Red, Leap Forward, Little Iron, and Little Steel. I am going to count to ten, and then we will release our kites. The kite that stays up the longest is the winner.'

Little-Little prepared his own kite, which was a diamond shape, with paper tails cascading from three corners. On the count of ten, we ran along the riverbank, releasing our kites when the pull of the wind seemed its strongest. It was a beautiful sight, as the white kites rose up into the sky. They all looked similar, but each one was slightly different: finer strips of bamboo perhaps, a different glue recipe, longer tails arranged in different ways, the

ends curved with scissors or cut like ribbons.

I admired the sight, but concentrated hard on controlling my own kite. It was twisting and turning in the wind. I unwound a good length of string quickly – giving my kite the freedom to soar higher and higher. I could feel its force tugging at my hand. Was it struggling to get away from my grasp, or did it want me to join it among the grey-white clouds? I looked up and felt myself lost in the sky, which was colourless and yet still piercingly bright.

Suddenly I felt a violent tugging on my hand: another kite had soared into mine. It was Little Iron's. He was looking at me and grinning. My kite lost its balance. I thought the paper was going to tear. I jerked my hand to move the string and my kite swerved to one side, still in one piece and flying.

There were only three kites left in the sky now, and I could feel the eyes of the group watching, to see whose kite would win. I felt a powerful gust of wind lifting my kite, and I unwound my string even more. I had to get the timing just right.

'Please keep going. Please keep going,' I whispered.

It soared and soared, its tails streaming, like a beautiful white bird heading for the stars. But two other kites were beside it.

'Oh no!' shouted Little-Little. 'I've run out of string!'

His kite was left, suspended in the sky, unable to go further.

The two remaining kites continued to soar, and I glanced over my shoulder to where Blue was standing with her friends. I wanted to make sure she was looking.

At that moment I lost my footing on the riverbank and stumbled to the ground – the bobbin still clutched firmly in my hand. My kite dropped into the branches of a Yang Shu tree.

I could hear Little-Little shouting:

'Little Iron is the winner! Bad luck Leap Forward. It's a pity he's not as agile as his name suggests!'

Everyone laughed, and at that moment I hated my friend. He had said it to get a laugh, to make the

others think he was clever. I tugged angrily at the limp string that was tangled among the heart-shaped leaves, but the kite was stuck fast in the tree and wouldn't move at all. I cut the bobbin free with my penknife, pushed it into the pocket of my jacket, and shrugged to show that I didn't care about my kite. Then I picked up a stone and hurled it into the river. I sat down on the riverbank and turned my back on the kite-flyers, waiting for them to leave.

I continued throwing stones until the riverbank was quiet behind me. Everyone had gone home. I turned to go too. But then I saw Blue leaning against a white tree trunk, eating an apple, the red silk ribbons on her plaits brightening the greyness of the afternoon.

'I thought your kite was the best,' she said, with a shy smile. 'I'm sorry you didn't win. I thought Little-Little was mean.'

'Thank you,' I said. 'He was just looking for a laugh.'

I tried to sound casual.

I picked up a smooth flat stone and sent it skimming six times across the river. I felt her dark eyes watching me.

'My mother was making noodles when I left my courtyard. Would you like to eat with us?'

'Yes please,' I said in surprise. 'I'd better tell my sisters though. Can you wait here for five or ten minutes and I'll be right back?'

She nodded her head and carried on eating her apple.

Running back to the alleys at full speed, I nearly knocked over my sister Victory, who was standing in our courtyard.

'I'm going to eat with a friend tonight,' I stammered, out of breath. 'Her name is Blue.'

'Isn't she the daughter of the newspaper journalist?' my sister asked, her eyes sparkling with amusement.

'Yes,' I shouted over my shoulder as I ran out of the courtyard, and back through the alleys to the river.

'You didn't have to run all the way,' Blue said, throwing her apple core into the river, and watching it bob away like a little boat. 'The noodles won't be ready yet. Come on. Let's walk slowly!'

We went over the little bridge to the other side of the river – outside the old part of Beijing – and along the path beside the wheat, which moved like a sea of silk in the early evening wind. I had forgotten my white kite, trapped in the branches of the Yang Shu tree, and we talked about other things, including Little Cloud.

'Have you learnt to whistle her song?' Blue asked me.

'She hasn't sung anything yet,' I replied, feeling my face turn red. 'She's still getting used to life in the courtyard, I think. It's very noisy, with musicians practising their instruments, and people coming and going all the time. But soon she'll sing, I'm sure. She takes a sunflower seed from my fingers, and I'm going to train her to sit on my hand.'

'I would love to see her,' Blue said.

We had reached her courtyard, and entered through a big gate with characters drawn on the wood in white chalk. It was a big modern compound

housing the families of journalists who worked for the 'Workers Newspaper' in Beijing, which was read by all the factory workers. It was a government policy, to put people of the same profession in courtyards together, like boxes of ingredients in a grocery shop. I had never been inside a writers' compound before, and had imagined the walls to be covered with newspapers – the black print still wet, rubbing off on my fingers – and the sound of a hundred tapping typewriters filling the air. I was not disappointed! There were big glass cases with sheets of newspaper on display – and the sound of voices and typewriters through open doors. But it was so vast and modern, compared to my small traditional courtyard.

'I can't imagine living with writers and not musicians,' I said.

Blue laughed.

'It must be nice to live with all that music around you! I just have the sound of my father's typewriter tapping away in the evening, when I'm going to sleep. Sometimes he works all through the night! But I don't mind – I quite like the rhythm of the tapping, and then the silence when he's thinking. But it's not musical!'

'My father used to say that you can find music anywhere, if you listen for it,' I said.

'I like that idea,' Blue replied.

Blue's mother welcomed me warmly, urging me to sit down and eat the handmade noodles, which we call 'flour ribbons'. Afterwards, we were each handed an apricot, the skin like pale-orange velvet. We ate the fruit, and drank from little blue cups filled with jasmine tea.

'Leap Forward,' Blue whispered when we had finished, 'I want to show you something before you go.'

She led me into the inner room, where a black shiny piano stood like a soldier, straight and polished. Pulling an old lacquer box from under the bed, she opened it with great care.

'It was my father's when he was a little boy,' she

said in a serious voice, taking out an old kite with frayed ribbon tails, and painted in many colours, all of which had faded over time.

'On this side there is a phoenix,' she said. 'My father says the phoenix stands for many things: its head is the sky, its back is the moon, its wings are the wind and its feet are the earth. The song of the phoenix includes all five notes of the Chinese musical scale. Wouldn't you love to hear it sing?'

I nodded, as she turned the kite gently in her hands.

'On the other side is a dragon – look, in red and gold. My father says that a dragon can disguise itself as a tiny silkworm; it can fly among the clouds, and turn itself into water or fire. And here there is poetry, but written in old characters: something about loyalty and honesty. Don't you think it's beautiful? Can you imagine it flying in the sky? I wish I could wear all those colours too – like girls used to. I've seen photographs of my grandmother – black and white of course. But still, you can see the patterns of flowers on her silk clothes, and the tiny

embroidered shoes that she wore on her bound feet –
and the butterfly combs in her hair. I love to imagine
all the different colours.'

The kite looked old and crumpled in her hands, as
if it might turn into dust at any moment. It was like
a faded butterfly, kept in a box; it seemed dead to me.
I preferred my own kites, after all – they were fresh
and white, and alive. But Blue's words were beautiful. She was a better poet than me; and I wanted to
make her happy.

'Yes,' I said, 'it is a beautiful kite.'

She looked up at me, with questioning eyes, and
then she smiled.

As I walked back through the field of wheat and
across the bridge, I looked up at the sky. It was dark
blue and vast. The wind had died down, and I no
longer minded about losing the kite competition. I
thought about Blue, about how I would show her
Little Cloud, my silkworms and my fish. I knew she
would understand.

CHAPTER SEVEN

MY BAMBOO FLUTE

THE NEXT EVENING, I WAITED AT THE END of the alley for my mother to come home from work. Her bus stop was further down the street, but even when it was getting dark I could always tell, among the crowds of people stepping off the bus, which was my mother, just by the way she moved and held her head. I ran to meet her.

'I was missing you Ma,' I said, taking her hand.

'How is my Leap Forward today?' she smiled, looking tired.

'I'm well Ma. I have been looking after Little Cloud; though Swallow and Whirlwind say I must stop giving her so many sunflower seeds.'

'And has she sung a note yet?' she laughed.

'Don't laugh Ma! I've been trying everything.'

'I'm sorry, Leap Forward,' she said. 'Perhaps I can think of something that might help her to sing.'

After dinner she knocked on the door of one of our neighbour's rooms in the courtyard. He was a musician who had once worked with my father. When she returned and sat down to her sewing she looked pleased.

'Tomorrow you are going to buy a bamboo flute, Leap Forward. I think you will like it, and Little Cloud too! Maybe it's just what you need to make her sing. And guess how I'm going to pay for your lessons? With a tiny bottle of peanut oil!' she laughed. 'Isn't that wonderful?'

She was still smiling later that evening as she sat on her bed, loosening her hair and sipping jasmine tea.

'I wish I could tell your father,' she said, blowing her tea to cool it down. 'He would have been so happy.'

The following afternoon, I ran to keep up with the

musician as he marched through the alleys towards the Red Flag Paper Shop. He was talking about my father.

'He was one of the best violinists in Beijing,' he told me, 'and a good cook too! I remember when he and your mother first moved to the courtyard he often used to cook for all the musicians and their families on a coal stove outside. With one potato, a cucumber and a carrot, he could make a feast that was fit for an Emperor! You could smell his cooking all through the alleys.'

Soon we were inside the Red Flag Paper Shop, making our way past the bamboo brushes and ink-stones, to a small collection of bamboo flutes. There were five or six small flutes, made from bare, natural bamboo – not painted like old Chinese flutes. There was no poetry written on them. But the colour – a reddish-golden-brown – and the scent of the bamboo were beautiful. The musician showed me how to place my fingers over the holes and how to blow to make a sound. This powerful sound was created by a tiny transparent paper, lighter than a dragonfly's wing, which covered the first hole of the flute and vibrated with the force of my breath. The paper was taken from one of the many layers inside a piece of bamboo. I chose the flute that had the brightest sound and carried it home inside a long box, covered in green flowery paper. That night I kept waking up to open the box – just to make sure my flute was still there.

'She's so lovely, Leap Forward,' Blue said, as she knelt down to give Little Cloud a piece of steamed bread through the bamboo frame of her cage. I had carried the cage into our inner room, so that Little-Little could not interrupt us.

'She looks like something out of a book or a painting. She's so tiny. Can I hold her?'

I had worked out the best way to handle Little Cloud. If I caught her attention by tapping a sunflower seed on one side of the cage, I could put my hand quickly through the door and pick her up without her seeing me. I knew just how tightly I could hold her, and she seemed more used to me now. She pecked at my hand as I held her, but with a gentle rhythm, as if searching for another seed, and I liked the feeling. Blue put her hands around mine, and I saw her face going pink. I let go of my hands gradually, so that she was holding Little Cloud by herself.

'She's so light!' she exclaimed. 'I can feel her heart beating. Isn't it amazing that we can hold something so wild in our hands.'

She held Little Cloud close to her for a while, before I put her gently back into the cage.

I showed Blue my silkworms too, which I kept in a box.

'Maybe one of these is really a dragon, that's turned itself into a silkworm!' she said.

We laughed.

'Here, you can have this.'

I handed her a circle of shiny silk. It was yellow, the natural colour that silk is before it's dyed another colour.

'Thank you, Leap Forward!' Blue said, stroking

the silk with her fingers. 'Did your silkworms really make it?'

'Yes – but not these ones; they're too little to make silk. This piece was made by the silkworms I had before. They worked all night to make it!' I said.

'But how?' Blue insisted, her eyes sparkling.

'Well, you have to fix a sheet of message-paper over the top of a rice bowl, using a rubber band, and then you put the fully-grown silkworms on to the paper. Soon they begin to move their heads, making the silk as if they are moving in time with music that we cannot hear. They make the silk right up to the edge of the paper: that's why it's a circle. My mother says that they keep on working, giving silk, until they have no more silk to give. Then they build themselves a cocoon.'

'And what happens inside the cocoon?'

'The silkworm goes to sleep I think, and changes. It's like it dies, and then it comes to life again, but this time it has wings. It changes into a big silk moth and flies away.'

'Maybe that's its reward, for making something so beautiful,' Blue said, holding the silk against her cheek.

'Maybe,' I said. 'But I think silkworms also have a good life when they're munching on mulberry leaves and getting fatter and fatter!'

'It sounds like you wouldn't mind being a silkworm, Leap Forward!' she laughed.

I showed her my fish too – orange, white, yellow and gold.

'They're lovely colours,' she said. 'I'd like to paint them. Can I, one day?'

I nodded.

'But do you think they get bored Leap Forward?' Blue asked me, gazing into the glass tank which Clear Waves had also helped me to build.

'They just swim in circles – never going anywhere.'

'You sound like Little-Little!' I laughed. 'Fish don't think, any more than birds or silkworms do.'

'How do you know that?' she asked.

I shrugged my shoulders.

'I just do,' I said. 'They can feel things – like the

water or the air. Maybe they see colours too. They have sensations. But they don't have thoughts or feelings like us.'

We sat in silence for a while.

'But we can't know that,' Blue insisted. 'Perhaps a bird sees the colour of a red berry or an empty blue sky and thinks it is beautiful; or perhaps it listens to the sound of the wind in the Yang Shu trees because it loves the sound. How do we know it doesn't have thoughts and feelings like us?'

I shrugged again, because I didn't know the answer.

'Do you want to see my flute?' I said instead, reaching for the green-flowered box and taking out the smooth reddish-gold bamboo. 'Or are you going to tell me that I shouldn't keep this in a box either!'

Blue laughed and settled down to listen. I played her the few scales I had learnt and a simple tune that the musician had taught me. When I had finished, Blue clapped her hands.

'Well, if I was Little Cloud,' she said, 'I would definitely sing after hearing your music! It's beautiful.'

CHAPTER EIGHT

THE RED GUARDS

A S THE WEEKS PASSED I PRACTISED my flute every day. Often I would go out into the courtyard early in the morning, with a tiny spoonful of the sticky rice soup I had for breakfast. When I put some on my finger, Little Cloud would peck gently at the white rice. She seemed to like it. Then, standing beside her cage, I would play my flute, hoping the sound might encourage her to sing, as my mother and Blue both thought. But still she didn't make a sound.

One morning, after feeding Little Cloud, I found my mother sitting on my sisters' bed in our inner room, looking through a box of old letters and photographs. Her favourite poetry books, from the Tang and Song dynasties, were also on the bed.

'What are you doing Ma?' I asked her.

She looked at me, and there was something in her dark eyes that reminded me of Little Cloud, the first time I held her in my hands on the riverbank.

'I'm just looking at the past, Leap Forward. It's a strange thing.'

I could see there were tears in her eyes.

'Tell me about how you used to go ice-skating in Harbin, Ma, and about your Russian friends.'

My mother had grown up near the border between China and Russia, and she spoke Russian fluently.

'I used to go ice-skating with my best friend, a Russian girl,' she said, her face brightening as she talked. 'She had golden hair and blue eyes – like a character in a Russian novel. Her name was Olga. She had a white fur coat. Wait.'

She was rummaging in the box, and eventually pulled out a black and white photograph of two girls, arm in arm, smiling and posing. The photograph was very faded, with writing on the back that I couldn't read.

'To my dearest friend,' my mother read, pointing to each Russian word as she translated it.

I was glad she was smiling again.

'I'm going to see Little Cloud now, Ma,' I said.

She looked up, but I don't think she saw me. I think she was back in Harbin – a beautiful girl, skating on the ice in a new fur coat. At the door I turned round again. She had a poetry book on her lap and was holding it very tightly with both hands.

Outside in the courtyard, I tapped on Little Cloud's cage and she fluttered her wings. It was true – they looked less golden than before. Or was it my imagination? I took a sunflower seed from my pocket, and held it out to her.

'Why won't you sing, Little Cloud?' I asked her. 'Please sing for me.'

She put her head on one side, as if listening for something.

I whistled to her, and she watched me with her

bright silent eyes. I fetched a grape from the vine that Clear Waves had planted in the courtyard, and Little Cloud pecked at the dark-purple skin. The red juice was running down my hand. I thought about getting my flute.

But then I felt another pair of dark eyes watching me, and turning, I saw Little-Little leaning against his door in the courtyard, his hands in his pockets. He caught my eye, and looked down at his cotton shoes.

'Do you want to come to the river, Leap Forward? Just to throw some stones,' he said, in a voice that was not quite like his own. 'Or we could think up another game if you like. I've got some ideas.'

'Alright,' I said, trying to sound casual.

We walked side by side down the alley, towards the river.

'I'm sorry about the kite competition, the thing I said. I didn't mean to. It just came out.'

I looked at Little-Little. He was walking along, looking at the ground. Suddenly he bent down to pick up a rubber band and an apricot stone, pushing them both into his pocket. I had missed my best friend. I gave him a push with both hands, and he laughed as he recovered his balance.

'Come on,' I said. 'I'll race you to the river.'

Soon we were throwing ourselves onto the riverbank again.

'Something big is happening, Leap Forward,' he said as we lay there, staring up at the blue sky and breathing hard. 'I heard my parents talking.'

I didn't answer, though I too had heard people talking in the alleys. They were talking quietly of 'counter-revolutionaries' – people who were against Chairman Mao and were going to be punished. I had never heard such quiet voices in the alleys before.

The birds were singing in the Yang Shu trees, and the heart-shaped leaves were still, as if frozen in a photograph. I sat up a bit, leaning back on my elbows. Dragonflies were skimming the water, like blurred ribbons of blue silk, and the golden wheat was motionless in the field beyond the bridge.

I thought about Blue's courtyard and the tapping of the typewriters.

We invented a game, digging holes in the earth with a stick, and then throwing the apricot stone into each hole. You had to have a steady hand and a good aim. Little-Little was also busy making a catapult with his rubber band. It was hot, and after a while we took off our shoes and waded around in the river, flicking cold water at each other. When hunger got the better of us, we made our way back to the alleys.

Afterwards, Little-Little said that the sound had been like thunder at the beginning of a storm. I thought it was more like an explosion. As we entered the alleys we saw army trucks full of students in army-green uniforms, with red armbands and black shining loudspeakers. The students were throwing little sheets of paper and shouting:

'Get rid of old China. Make a new China.'

Some of the students had sticks and were smashing old windows and the faded grey tiles that

had old Chinese poetry written on them. We could see people being marched out of their courtyards, with their hands forced behind their backs. Little-Little picked up one of the paper sheets and began reading the printed characters; but I got hold of his sleeve and pulled him towards our courtyard.

'Revolution is about one class taking over another class,' he read. 'What do you think those people have done?'

'I don't know,' I replied. But I was shaking.

The courtyard was empty and we sat on the steps, waiting for someone to come. Little-Little's eyes were dark with fear. I got Little Cloud's cage down from the tree and put it on the steps beside us. She was flying frantically from one side of the cage to the other. The noises must have scared her. I was afraid she might hurt her wings against the bamboo sticks, and I tried to soothe her, whispering words and whistling tunes I thought she liked. Gradually she became still again, even taking some grain from Little-Little's fingers.

'You know she's never going to sing, Leap Forward,' he said in a dull voice. 'She doesn't belong here.'

I didn't say anything.

'I wish I'd never caught her,' he said, staring at his feet again.

'But I can keep her safe,' I said. 'I won't let anything bad happen to her.'

Little-Little looked at me.

'Wouldn't you rather be free, just for a day, than spend a lifetime in a cage?'

The next morning my sisters told me that Clear Waves had stayed up all night and had burned my mother's letters, photographs and books, one by one, in our painted-metal washing-basin. I thought about the poetry book that my mother had held so tightly, and the look I had seen in her eyes, and the photograph of her Russian friend. I was trying to understand.

'It's very dangerous to love the old things of China now, Leap Forward, or to love foreign things,'

my sister Swallow tried to explain. 'It's not safe to have come from a wealthy background, like Ma. The Red Guards – those students with loudspeakers – are against anyone who criticises the Revolution. They want only a new China now.'

I sat on the steps with Little-Little and Little Cloud.

'My father says many things are being banned,' Little-Little said. 'Books, poetry, art, music, even playing chess in tea-houses, or keeping cats and dogs as pets – anything that isn't revolutionary. You are not even allowed to fly kites in Tiananmen Square!'

'You mean we can't fly our kites any more?'

Little-Little shrugged. 'I don't think the Red Guards are going to bother with us. Not by the river anyway.'

It was called the Cultural Revolution – the Red Guards swarming through the streets and alleys, the burning of books and the banning of kites and old poetry. Soon after it began, our school was closed.

I had not seen Blue for many days. But one afternoon she came to our courtyard. Her long black plaits had been cut short and her red silk ribbons were gone.

'The Red Guards are cutting women's hair and the heels of their shoes as they step off the buses, Leap Forward!' she said. 'They are not allowed to wear make-up or pretty scarves any more. It is not revolutionary. But look!'

She pulled down the collar of her blue cotton jacket, and showed me a red silk ribbon, which she had tied round her neck and fastened with a bow.

'No one can see it,' she said.

'I still have the piece of silk you gave me too.'

She looked at me and smiled. Then her gaze wandered to Little Cloud's cage.

'The Red Guards burned my father's books you know.'

I looked at her, not knowing what to say.

'And his kite.'

She looked down at her black cotton shoes.

'I'm glad you saw it,' she said quietly.

Before she left, she poked a red berry from her pocket into Little Cloud's cage, and I promised to go to her courtyard soon.

CHAPTER NINE

INTO THE SKY

A FEW DAYS LATER I FOUND Little-Little standing outside his door, holding a new white kite. It was small and shaped like a diamond, with the longest tails I had ever seen. Even in the courtyard, the wind was already rattling the thin message paper, with its faint red lines. It seemed impatient.

'This is my best one yet, Leap Forward,' Little-Little declared. 'It's going to fly higher than any kite ever before! Are you coming to see it?'

'I don't know Little-Little. I was going to practise my flute. I have to hold each long note for a whole minute. That's a long time when you are holding your breath you know!'

'So bring your flute to the river. The air is clearer there.'

We walked quickly through the alleys, with our heads down, Little-Little holding his kite under his blue jacket. But no one took any notice of us. Soon we were on the riverbank, away from the trucks and loudspeakers.

'You can play while I fly my kite,' Little-Little said.

Unfolding the tails, he carefully smoothed them out. They were already rippling in the wind. Unwinding the string, he ran along the riverbank until a gust of wind lifted his kite and he let it go.

'Look Leap Forward!' he shouted, 'I told you it was the best one I ever made.'

We watched the kite as it soared above the river, wrestling with the wind to get its balance. As it rose higher and higher, I picked up my flute and began to play – not the scales and revolutionary tunes I was now being taught, but something else, a melody that came from inside me, a tune that seemed in keeping with the Yang Shu trees and the dragonflies –

something winding and soaring – something free.

'Keep playing Leap Forward,' Little-Little shouted. 'Look, it's still going higher.'

I looked up into the sky as I played, moving my body in time with the kite. It seemed as high as the clouds now, its red lines dissolved in the blueness of the sky. It looked as if it was searching for something, no longer struggling as my mother had described. But then, as Little-Little unwound his string to the end, it stopped moving and twisting, and seemed just to hover among the small white clouds, to be almost still, high above the earth.

'Look Leap Forward,' Little-Little kept shouting. 'I've never gone that high before. It's not tugging now.'

I looked up, and stopped playing my flute. Suddenly I thought about Little Cloud. What would it feel like to fly so high, and then to never fly again? Did she remember? Was that why she wouldn't sing?

I looked across at Little-Little. He looked at me and shouted:

'Have you ever seen a better kite Leap Forward?'

I shook my head.

Then suddenly he let go of the string. We both looked up as the kite was carried away by the wind. It was just a white dot in the sky. And then it was nothing.

'Why did you do that?' I asked.

He shrugged his shoulders, but kept looking at the sky.

'Let's go home,' he said.

Back in the courtyard, I found my sister Swallow standing quietly in front of Little Cloud's cage, giving her a sunflower seed. Like Blue, her plaits had been cut short and were tied with rubber bands. Her green army cap had a red star on the front. When she saw us, she quickly brushed her cheek with the back of her hand.

'She is very beautiful Leap Forward. I can see why you love her,' she laughed. 'Oh,' she called back over her shoulder as she walked into the outer room. 'I heard today that Blue has been sent to the countryside, to live with her grandmother. Her father thought it was too dangerous for her to stay in Beijing.'

I felt as if something had hit me hard in the stomach.

Blue – whose silk ribbons brightened the greyness of the alleys.

I wanted to talk to her, to tell her something.

I felt Little-Little's hand on my shoulder.

'I'm in my room if you want me, Leap Forward,' he said quietly.

I went up to Little Cloud's cage and stood there, gazing at the soft feathers and dark eyes that Blue had thought were like a painting. She seemed even smaller than before.

'Are you missing the sky too much Little Cloud? Is that why you can't sing? Is that what you wanted to tell me?'

Her dark eyes were watching me.

'I love you,' I whispered.

Slowly, I lifted the wire handle from the tree.

'Let's go,' I said.

Lifting the cage into my arms, I left the courtyard. Through the narrow alleys, past the grocery shop, past many bicycles and courtyards, I made my way towards the dragonflies and the Yang Shu trees. I looked down at Little Cloud. She was darting from one side of the cage to the other, tilting her head and listening.

Resting her cage on the riverbank, I sat down to look at her. I wanted to remember everything: her lightness, the darkness of her eyes, the shape of her head, and the feathers that shone like gold again in the sunshine. Slowly I opened the bamboo door.

'Look, Little Cloud!' I whispered. 'You're free now. You can fly!'

For a moment she seemed to hesitate.

Perhaps she would stay. I could close the door – there was still time. I could take her back to the courtyard and we could carry on – just the same. But then I thought about Blue, and the faded kite she had held so gently in her hands. What would she say?

'It's all right, Little Cloud,' I said. 'You can go now. I understand.'

There was a shimmer of gold as she lifted her wings – and I felt something brush, like a whisper, against my hand. Looking up, I could see nothing except the piercing sunshine that made my eyes stream with tears.

'Leap Forward!'

My friend Little-Little was running along the riverbank towards me.

'Did you let her go?'

He was breathing hard.

'You did the right thing,' he said.

'What do you know?' I said angrily, wiping my face with my sleeve.

'My mother said I should give this to you,' he shrugged, handing me a letter. 'Someone brought it to the courtyard. Do you want it or not?'

I took the letter from his hand and opened it. Inside was a sheet of white paper, with characters written

neatly on the red lines, and a red silk ribbon that fell
from the envelope on to the earth.

'I don't have time to say goodbye Leap Forward –
only to give you this. I hope you will remember me
– whenever you see a kite, soaring in the sky.'

I bent down and picked up Blue's red ribbon. I put
it in my pocket.

'Come on Leap Forward,' Little-Little said.

'Let's go.'

CHAPTER TEN

AUTUMN SONG

A FEW WEEKS LATER MY MOTHER came into the inner room where I was practising my bamboo flute. She was holding a cardboard box in her arms.

'Leap Forward. Someone in the alleys just gave me this for you.'

I looked inside. The box was full of mulberry leaves and tiny new silkworms.

'Thank you, Ma!' I said.

'That's the first time I've seen you smile in weeks,' she said, sitting down on my sisters' bed.

I looked down at my flute.

'Don't you go to the river any more Leap Forward?' she asked.

'Swallow says you are always in here by yourself, practising your flute.'

'I want to get my scales and long notes right,' I said. 'I want to be as fast as Swallow is, when she is chopping vegetables!'

My mother smiled.

'But what happened to the boy who was going to write music for his silkworms to dance to?' she asked.

'That was your idea, Ma!' I laughed.

'Was it?' she replied. 'Well I think it's a good idea.'

'Maybe, Ma,' I said.

'But I don't think you're going to find your music here, in the alleys and courtyards.'

'Maybe I can't find it at all,' I said – 'not even by the river.'

'Perhaps. But if you don't try, you will never know,' she said.

I had almost forgotten how calm and beautiful the river was, especially now that late summer was turning into autumn. The trunks of the Yang Shu trees were as white as snow in the bright sunlight, and the sky seemed endlessly blue. I lay down on the riverbank, staring up into the sky. I wanted to lose myself in it. Then I remembered my mother's words and sitting up, I began to finger the notes on my flute. I tried to remember the melody I had played, when Little-Little was flying his small white kite.

Suddenly I heard a sound above my head – a clear, sweet sound that rippled like silk through the quiet air. I looked up, but the sun was too bright and I couldn't see anything beyond the vivid green of the leaves. Then I heard the sound again – but closer to me. There, on the riverbank, was a little bird – tiny, with golden feathers and dark bright eyes. She was singing.

'Little Cloud?' I whispered, afraid that I would startle her, and she would fly away.

But instead she came closer.

I reached instinctively into my pocket and found a sunflower seed I had left there weeks ago.

'Here, Little Cloud,' I said. 'It's for you. Do you remember?'

The tiny bird fluttered her wings. The next moment I felt her on my hand, taking the seed. I looked down, trying not to move at all. A tiny red berry lay in the palm of my hand. She was watching me, her head tilted to one side.

'Darling Little Cloud,' I said. 'Thank you.'

She seemed to hesitate.

I bent my head and kissed her.

Her wings brushed my hand as she flew to the other side of the riverbank. Then she began to sing.

I put the berry in my pocket and picking up my flute I began to play, feeling for the notes that she was singing, trying to imitate the soaring patterns and freedom of her music. Her singing was beautiful, in the same way that the moon and stars are beautiful – in a way that words cannot really describe. Her music lifted my spirit and I searched for the right notes, willing myself to remember them.

I played for a long time until, absorbed in my

own music, I realised that Little Cloud was no longer there.

'Leap Forward, you're here!'

Little-Little flung himself on to the riverbank, out of breath and pulling off his black cotton shoes.

'Are you practising?' he asked.

'I've just finished,' I said. I looked at my friend and smiled. 'Do you want to skim some stones?' I asked him.

He looked at me seriously for a moment, and then a broad grin stretched wide across his face. 'I know!' he shouted. 'Let's have a competition!'

AFTERWORD

THIS STORY WAS INSPIRED BY THE events and characters of my early childhood in China.

I was born in 1958 and grew up as the son of a musician in a traditional courtyard in the north-east alleys (*hutongs*) of Beijing, near the fifteenth-century Drum and Bell Towers. My father had studied the *erhu* (the Chinese two-stringed violin) in a music conservatoire and my mother had studied economics at Beijing University. They had met in Chengdu, in the Sichuan Province. When Mao Zedong became leader of the Communist Party and founded the People's Republic of China in 1949, he introduced socialist thinking, inspired by Russia's Revolution of 1917. Mao was from a poor family in the countryside and did not trust intellectuals (people with

Yue as a boy in the Beijing alleys

knowledge and education). He believed that land should be taken away from rich landowners and that the countryside should be divided into communes – groups of peasants working and living together. He thought everyone should be the same.

He brought musicians from the countryside to Beijing and introduced them as 'treasures from the countryside'. These were poor, untrained musicians who had never learnt to read or write music, but they could play revolutionary tunes with a passion that made a huge impression on me as a child. Little-Little's father was one of these musicians. The Communist Party was very clever in using music and singing to influence people's thinking.

The Cultural Revolution, which began in Beijing on the 18th August 1966, was a further, disastrous step in Mao's thinking: he wanted to punish intellectuals, artists, writers, composers, people from wealthy backgrounds, and anyone who criticised him. A few months after the Cultural Revolution started, my mother was accused of being a 'counter-revolutionary' and was sent by the Red Guards to the countryside to be 're-educated'. She had to dig heavy mud out of a river and work like a

Yue with his sister Whirlwind, holding Mao's Little Red Book at the beginning of the Cultural Revolution

peasant farmer in the fields. Every day she was publicly criticised. She remained in the countryside for nearly three years. Only her spirit was not broken.

In the second year of the Cultural Revolution Little-Little and Little Stone were sent by their parents, like Blue, to the countryside,

Yue (right) with his best friend Xiao-Xiao (left) in their courtyard

117

Yue playing his di-zi
(bamboo flute) with his brother
Art playing the sheng

to live with their grandparents – away from the centre of the Revolution in Beijing. I never saw them again.

Three of my sisters, including Swallow, were also sent to the countryside. I remained in the courtyard with my brother Art and my first sister Victory, who married Clear Waves. I missed my mother so much, and put all my feeling into playing the bamboo flute. I wanted her to be proud of me.

When my mother returned to Beijing she suffered a series of strokes, and gradually lost the powers of movement and speech. She had suffered too much. For many years she remained still and silent, like a silkworm in its cocoon. She died in 1994.

At the age of seventeen I successfully auditioned for an army dancing and singing ensemble, and performed throughout China on the bamboo flutes and the silver flute. I loved my instruments, and being on stage. But still, I wanted to be free.

In 1976, Mao Zedong died; but the Communist Party remained in power. In 1981, my sister Swallow was walking up a mountain with friends and met a Frenchman: after much difficulty, because he was a foreigner, they were married and left China. The following year she applied for me to study the silver flute at the Guildhall School of Music in London. In 1982, aged twenty-three, I left my courtyard and travelled to England. I wanted to write and perform the music that was in my heart. Since then, I have played my bamboo flutes to audiences all over the world.

Yue with his mother in the courtyard

LITTLE LEAP FORWARD

In May 1994 I saw a girl, looking into a glass case of turquoise jewellery. The stones were the same colour as the sky above the river in my Beijing childhood. Around her neck she wore a small gold star, studded with tiny white pearls, on a white silk ribbon. When we talked, it was as if we had always known each other. We loved the same things: poetry, music and art. Now, many years later, we have two children: a son called North Sound, and a daughter, Blue Sky.

In 2005, I returned to China, to record some traditional Chinese music to accompany the book that I have written with Clare, called *Music, Food and Love* – the story of my childhood. In a Beijing market, early one morning, I found a white jade flute. Its sound was simple, timeless and beautiful. I have called it Little Cloud.

A Note on Chinese Names
Guo Yue is referred to as 'Yue' because this is his first name. In China the order is reversed.

120